CREDIT REPAIR FRAUD

WHAT LAW SAYS YOU HAVE TO PAY A BILL?

ENVI

CONTENTS

ASK QUESTIONS

I am not your average author ~ Envi

Everyone by now has heard of credit repair. Credit repair is a term that is very miss commonly used. Most would say credit repair is something to help you get what you want out of life such as a car house or boat etc. Well, every time I asked someone that question what is credit repair they tell me that so I know for a fact they have not read any laws pertaining to their business. Now of course this will ruffle some feathers, but the truth hurts anybody if they are living the lie. After years of studying, working with thousands of clients and going on a nationwide tour helping others gain freedom it was time to reach more.

Many people know me from social media and they adore how I breakdown everything. For example, the term credit repair on its own sounds weird if you think about it. Again, if you ask a credit repair agent what is credit they may tell you credit is something that you need in order to gain what you want in life. That is the wrong answer ladies and gentlemen. Now let us look at the word repair when did you break your credit? In order for something to be repaired that mean it had to be whole at one point of time but they also tell you to build credit so is it whole or something you buil, lol they are confused trust me.

Credit is something that never had to be built as we were taught we will get into those details a little bit later. One of the most darndest things these credit repair agents tell you is to pay upfront or they have some sort of payment arrangement for you.

That is your first red flag when they ask you for payment whether it is up front or during the process. Pursuant to the credit repair organization act, it is illegal and against federal law to collect payment before all services are performed. The law states you can sue anybody who offered you services to repair your credit even if they do not have a business. Some of these huge credit repair companies know these laws and will put a disclaimer on their website stating they cannot charge you upfront but will create a payment arrangement for you so you don't pay it all at once but that is illegal too. All services MUST be completed before payment is made. They cannot have you sign power of attorney; they cannot mention they can sweep your credit, improve your credit and not even mention increasing a credit score. Go look it up under 15 USC 1679(b). Another question I like to ask a credit repair agent is can you please show me a law where I am obligated as a consumer to pay a debt.

Now that term consumer may be foreign to most of you but pursuant to federal law that term is one you may want to know and completely comprehend. The term consumer is a natural person under federal law 15 USC 1692a(3).

Now I want you all to brace yourself for the next few chapters you are going to read many of you have probably read some of these laws and did not understand and most of you have probably never heard of the laws. Nine times out of ten, when I am having a casual conversation in a public setting like the mall or a hair salon people look at me like I am crazy because they have never read these laws that is how mindboggling this knowledge is and why they never teach this in school. Think about it, once you do more research and see exactly what the law states it will make you think why they did not teach us this. They taught us the exact opposite such as how to budget, pay on a credit card and balance a checkbook. They never taught us what exactly credit was but quickly offered us a credit card as freshman in college or as soon as we turned 18. Under federal law, the term credit card is so far left from what they said or taught us. (Under truth in lending act). Most teens are excited to get a driver's license because they were taught it is required by law to drive. Well, if you are one of those people then you should not have a problem understanding what the law says (in a way lol). None of these laws I've made up and they are all PUBLIC LAWS so if you feel they are wrong communicate that with the ones who wrote them.

CONSUMER PROTECTION

Now let us into the nitty gritty. There are set of laws called consumer protection laws under the United states code Title 15 Chapter 41. My famous question I always ask is what law says you must pay a bill? No one has probably ever asked you that question and you have probably never even thought about it. Think about it right now take one minute and think about one law that says you are obligated to pay a bill. Again, I am very particular with words I don't even like calling it a "bill" because when you look up that term "bill" that means a law or a part belonging to a bird. Let us move on, have you found any laws that pertain to a natural person that state they are obligated to pay debt? Now let me clarify the term debt. Again, if you ask the average person what debt is they are going to say something that you haven't paid that you owe. That is the wrong answer again ladies and gentlemen let me clarify what the federal law says about the term debt. Under the definitions listed under the fair debt collection practices act, the term debt means "any obligation or alleged obligation of a consumer to pay money arising out of a transaction in which the money property insurance or services which are the subject of the transaction are primarily for personal family or household purposes whether or not such obligation has been reduced to judgment". Now the average set of eyes would read that and be a little bit confused so let me clarify it. The first thing you will notice it says any obligation "or". When "or" is used in a sentence some things it is up for grabs. It says *any* obligation or *alleged* obligation did you get that?

So technically debt is a twofold word it is any obligation or an alleged obligation. Which one you will choose; you can't be both. So, again the average person saying debt means money now should know differently; a*ny obligation* so think of this as anything anyone obligating you to perform or do such without your direct consent. Let us take the "bill" as an example, when you called your utility company to get your utilities turned it on did you request them to send you a bill or did you call to get your services set up? Now some of you may say, oh they asked me if I wanted paperless billing so technically, I did ask. If that's the case, did you say I will pay it as soon as you send the bill? Now we know people are going to challenge things so if you feel like you told your utility company you would pay, I want you to pay attention later on when we get into the laws. **DO YOU EVEN KNOW WHAT PAYMENT IS?**

Now that you know what debt is, I want you to go back to the original question: how can you repair something that is not broken? The next thing we need to do is clarify what credit is. I have not found one person to answer this correctly that is in the credit repair business or any other natural person. The majority will tell you credit is something you can get from a company like Visa, MasterCard, Discover or a bank, things of that nature and it is attached to a credit score (yawns). The consumer protection laws that go into this matter in detail is called the Truth in lending act. Think about that term truth in lending they want you to know who's doing the lending and what the truth is when it comes to credit. With all these consumer protection laws clarity is in their title alone. I always stress the congressional findings and purpose of every set of laws you read. Look at fair debt collection practices act (FDCPA) it looks like a set of laws that want you to see what is fair when it comes to debt collection. Congress said under 15 USC 1692 the existing laws in place were not working so they enacted the FDCPA , along with evidence of deceptive and misleading practices among consumers (that is you reading). Let's get back to credit, the truth in lending laws define the term credit as defined "the right granted by a creditor to a debtor". So you must be thinking at this moment oh that's when I go to apply for VISA. WRONG ANSWER!!!

Another famous quote I'm known for is, "if you know who you are you know what to do" but 90% of people do not know who they are. (I just made up that number I know it's a hella lot of people though). Let me take you back to the FDCPA. Under the FDCPA definitions, there is another term you should become familiar with which is creditor. The term "creditor" means any person who offers or extends credit creating a debt but that term does not include such person to the extent that he receives an assignment or transfer of a debt in default solely for the purpose of facilitating collection of such debts for another.

Let us look at the first half of that definition any person who offers or extends credit creating a debt. When you walk into a realtor office, boat dealership etc, you fill out a CREDIT APPLICATION but somehow they gave you a loan? Did that ever occur to you? The definition clearly states "offers or extends credit creating a debt". Who created the debt???? Back to the application, you filled out a CREDIT APPLICATION, created a debt but you are a borrower with a loan? Do that make sense? You did not fill out a loan application, federal law says the one creating the debt is the creditor so where did they get borrower from? If you search the federal consumer laws you will not find the term borrower as a natural person. Under the FDCPA the term borrower is not even defined so where is the term borrower under federal law!?!? All debt collectors are governed under the fair debt collection practices act so they are using a term not legally defined what do you think that mean? Think to yourself on that one. That term debt collectors is defined under the FDCPA as well under 15 USC 1692a.

FRAUD IS FRAUD

Why do I title this credit repair fraud? I think we've already clarified what credit is repair is. A common term where illegal actions are commonly used and known for ill gotten gain. One thing credit repair agents tell consumers to do is make payments on an account when the definition of debt clearly said alleged. When something is alleged it must be proven if you read further into the fair debt collection practices act you will find the answer to how it must be proven and how they never will prove it per federal law and owe you monetary compensation. Another thing your credit repair agent may have you believing is that you are a borrower as I mentioned earlier the term borrower is not even defined under the FDCPA that ALL debt collectors are governed under therefore that term makes everything null and void. Due to the fact under process of elimination the consumer the natural person is the only true creditor as they are the one that creates the debt per federal law along with other laws you can research after the bankruptcy of 1933.

There are several other public laws, house joint resolutions, congressional records, and case law regarding the inability of any bank or anyone other than a natural person ability to lend credit or have credit to lend.

During my nationwide tours I go into more details regarding where the credit is derived from and why the natural person is the only one with the power to possess unlimited credit. Another famous question I always ask credit repair agents, Can please explain to me what a credit score is per federal law and show me the law that says it is required for a consumer credit transaction? The look on their face is priceless. As you know they never know the answer they just say everybody gotta have one. Here recently U.S bank, Wells Fargo and other banks will no longer require credit scores. Let me take you back to the beginning with the driver's license scenario most people can tell you why they need a driver's license they can even probably tell you where and how to even get one and all the necessary things to go with that. But professionals credit prepare agents have no clue what a credit score is lawfully but they are attempting to make the natural person increase a ghost set of numbers and pay them thousands to do it. Sounds like a fraud to me.

Think about this if you own a business is it fair for you to be forced to pay? You own and create everything in that restaurant it makes no sense for you to be forced to pay for it, same logic with your credit the credit is yours it belongs to you it is your right per federal law so why do you have to apply for it and have a certain set of numbers for you to obtain it. THIS IS AMERICA!

Think people think!! Before you get upset and angry start with yourself because you did not know. You cannot be upset with these laws because you failed to educate yourself in a business that you wanted to call yourself a professional and you are committing fraud. Ignorance to the law is no excuse. Some may feel like I should not share the awareness of public laws due to the fact it may damage their business and character, but that is none of my business on how public laws make you feel. When the film "What the health" came out half of the world went crazy because they disagreed with facts or they did not want to see the truth being exposed. The dairy and meat industry declined quickly. The truth shall set you free! That is just a tip of the iceberg when it comes to the credit repair business and the fraud they commit knowingly and willingly due to the laws being public.

I have not even mentioned the fair credit reporting act also known as the FCRA. I still have not met a credit repair agent that has even read the fair credit reporting act if they even read that act alone they would know their job is useless on what they've been taught because it's fraud AND CONGRESS SAID IT! They're basically encouraging consumers to pay their own money back to the fraudsters vs understanding federal law of any person sending you a "bill" or any obligation is in violation of your consumer rights. Even under the United States Postal Service law (federal) debt collectors commit mail fraud. Everyone is a debt collector if they are collecting a debt, always in the business of collecting a debt, attempting to collect a debt. A fine is an example of an obligation which is a debt, the person who obligated you to the fine is the debt collector based on the attempt to collect a debt (your utility or any bills). Also, under the FCRA, congress explains how Equifax and them(credit reporting agencies) are committing fraud and they are not created by the government.

On my tours I really dive deep into the credit reporting agencies (there are over 400). The FDCPA is filled with so many remedies to help cure the common issues among consumers. One of my favorite sections is 15 USC 1692(e), that section is titled False or Misleading Representations. Under that section, it tells you "the false representation or implication that any individual is an attorney or that any communication is from an attorney". Let me break that down. The section is titled False and Misleading, and any attorney is not an attorney as they say they are or portray to be. So what does that tell you? YOU CANNOT BE SUED IF AN ATTORNEY IS INVOLVED... If one receives any paperwork from an "attorney" the law states otherwise about their status about being an attorney per federal law. I do not care about any BAR memberships, law school degrees because the federal law is clear ISSA FRAUD. You can argue all day, be in your feelings, disagree but if you do not have a federal law that rebuts that statement HUSH. Federal law trumps all laws. I do not want to even touch the CONSTITUTION (there are 2). Under the FDCPA it tells you no one is exempt from these laws and the FDCPA is supreme to any other laws that do not serve your greater protection as a consumer.

MONEY BAG TOUR

There is so much more I can go in detail about, but you will be more confused than you are now lol. The money bag tour was a one of a kind never seen before tour. I provided clarity on federal consumer protection laws and clarified how you are always entitled to get the money bag. One may say " That's legal advice" . My response is I am authorized to enlighten the people via my ancestors, and nothing is ever legal but lawful I shall say. Under the FDCPA, it states legal proceedings are false and misleading, especially if one is wearing a uniform or badge acting as if they are officers of the United States with authority. Yes, when I went on tour from 2019-2020 (thanks to COVID) my tour was called the Money Bag Tour. I completed the following cities: Raleigh, NC, Atlanta GA, Orlando, FL, and Columbus OH. March 2020 everything shut down with COVID- 19. I hope this knowledge jumpstart your beginning of research and a new lifestyle. We are creditors and the federal laws back us up if we utterly understand the laws that protect us and allow us to enforce these laws. Yes, enforce for any amount no cap! During my tours, we dive deep into Title 15 chapter 41 step by step. Since COVID-19 shut down my tour temporarily, the ancestors guided me to create my own online university. I did just that it is called SCALE INC ACADEMY. I pre-recorded videos with the public laws and provide the same clarity I did on my tours. One thing I will not do is provide templates for others to copy and paste. I refuse to handicap people again. I know hundreds of people that sell templates just to get a dollar. As I always say, if you know who you are you know what to do. It is much easier to study, comprehend then act vs panicking because you are not educated on laws and looking for someone to help you get your house, car or whatever back. Most of those people fail in life. That mindset of monkey see, monkey do is at an all-time high nowadays. No situation is the same so you will fail doing what someone told you what to do vs making informed decisions about situations you created.

People have to come to a point in life where they accept responsibility and make wise choices. I have never and never will tell someone not to pay something. I encourage people to study and do what they feel comfortable with. There are not many people out here truly trying to educate the people the right way. There are dozens of private FB groups declaring remedy for years. They make it seem as if there is some secret sauce and they are the only ones that know. It's time up for fraud amongst our people. I see real estate agents speaking NOTHING on the consumers rights when it comes to recission and even regulation B. Why because it taps into their money, they are not worried about you! They want commission period. Even under the Fair Housing Act they mention the illegal act that real estate agent participates in when a consumer want to view a high priced property JUST TO VIEW IT. That act says you CANNOT make housing unavailable when a consumer is purchasing a home. When they ask for a letter from bank verifying funds that is against federal law if you ask a real estate agent they should tell you the truth it is a common practice not legal. That is just the beginning of "real estate" fraud. I receive messages from people who taken my courses, even came to my tours and still afraid to act or embarrassed because of what others think. If your friends and family want to make fun of you because you chose to get educated, then that is their loss. Ask them to show you federal laws that say otherwise THEY CANNOT I PROMISE YOU. People will say anything to sway one from progressing in life. Those are the ones you need to separate from. Even if you believe you are wealthy you are probably not if you are counting Federal Reserve Notes or even what you think are assets (check electronic funds transfer act). That is a whole different topic for another book.

Americans have been depending on others to long to get results they desire then get the short end of the stick. I have seen so many times where people get "credit sweeps" and don't get any compensation as the law requires and they always get a letter from the so called creditor saying even though the account has been removed you are still responsible for the debt. You played yourself because you were not educated, you ASSUMED the credit repair company was going to help you get debt free before purchasing your new home, now it is 6 months later and you have to pay the debt anyway. Kill the ROOT KILLS THE PROBLEM. The debt is the ROOT. Everything comes from within. You must study and be diligent when it comes to changing your life for the better. Many of my clients have not paid any bills in years, winning lawsuits, getting homes back that was foreclosed on, and collecting checks from debt collectors like clockwork. I have had clients that cannot speak due to non-disclosures signed but collected checks in the millions. Many are gaining more confidence to be more assertive in situations and some just turned their nose up because they are comfortable being slaves. Then of course there are others who lack confidence and refuse to put the time in to study and throw tantrums like kids and say "those laws do not work" A slave is anyone under the control of another against your will. If you are paying any debt or being obligated to do anything you did not consent to you have a slave mentality. Once, this client said" I been paying all this time how will they look at me?" My response was WHAT LAW SAID YOU WERE OBLIGATED TO PAY! In any other situation where money or property was stolen and you find out who the perpetrator was you will go find them and probably get angry, yell, even use what they call profanity (lol) or probably get physical. Some may go the easier route and call the police and or have charges pressed on the individual. Either way you are willing to act. Keep that same energy when it's time to enforce your rights against these debt collectors. (pay attention to 15 USC 1692(e) they mention debt collectors that wear badges and uniforms).

All people are in fear of is a piece of paper. People are

afraid to open the mail, they get nervous as if that paper can do something. Think about this, BEST BUY, MACY'S, TOYOTA and any other corporation cannot talk! They are entities! The CEO or GM cannot testify to any matter without an attorney but the FDCPA says attorneys are fraud, so you know what that mean?!?! There is so much more to include but it is much better if you take the courses or catch a tour in the future.

Consumer protection laws are the only set of laws that protect you the natural person and your credit so why not use them. You are the sole one in charge pursuant to 15 USC 1692c(d). When I say no cap on monetary damages it is the truth just go to 15 USC 1692k. Hence, the reason for calling my tour THE MONEY BAG TOUR. You literally can collect a bag for everything they do (debt collectors). My clients have learned to dissect a collection letter and or bill and turn it into over $5000 for violations. From the time they send you something via mail to them attempting to garnish wages, repossess car etc they violate your consumer rights but yall want to fuss over civil rights. They cannot even talk to you NOBODY (15 USC 1692c(a)) without your DIRECT consent not INDIRECT. For example, you are served with child support paperwork. Did you personally go to the child support office and give them all your PRIVATE identifying information? Or did someone else give it to them? If someone has your private info such as name, address, social security ACCOUNT number without your direct consent that sounds like ID theft to me and is confirmed under the Fair Credit Reporting Act. They also did not have your consent to contact you and hire another agent to serve you. Another set of laws we clarify is known as the Equal Credit Opportunity Act, Electronic Funds Transfer Act, Fair Credit Billing act, Telephone Consumer Protection act and more. When violations (crimes) occur, there are a set of laws that outline they crime committed with jail time and stiff penalties. For example, Title 18 of the United States Code lists ALL crimes, and one is under Chapter 43. False personation is a crime involving citizens of the United States, officers or employees of the United States, Creditors of the United States. That coincides directly with the FDCPA 15 USC 1692e. That equates to imprisonment not more than 5 years. There are 123 chapters of crimes under title 18 I am sure you will find some to enforce.

I know this sound intimidating but there is nothing you cannot do. Who going to check you? A U.S citizen? That is impossible when there are congressional records that say the 14th amendment was never ratified in the Georgia State Archives. Facebook, Myspace, Blackplanet, Instagram, TIKtok and other social media platforms were nothing like you've seen before and now it has has created an entire career: SOCIAL MEDIA MANAGER. Prayer and meditation help you with scattered brain. Take time, clear your energy, drink water and breath and just study at least 30 min a day 3x a week or more. It is your life, and up to you on how you want to live it. If you choose to struggle paycheck to paycheck, always penny pinching that go ahead just do not complain when you tired of doing it and stop asking people for money to help pay your bills. People swear they INDEPEENDENT, they call themselves Queens and Kings but still a slave to 28 USC 3002(15) aka The United States Corporation.

I remember seeing all these Hollywood stars in trouble with the IRS for back taxes. That is when I knew something was wrong and these celebrities were getting pimped by their accountants and or lawyers. An accountant should know the difference between positive and negative right?!? Well how can one owe something in a positive amount? Have you ever seen a ledger and notice there are 2 sides? I mean it is common math taught in Elementary School. For example, If I open my bank account online and I owe the bank $300 it will say -$300. Now if I have $300 in the bank it will show $300 right! So, if you owed a bill why is it in a positive amount? The FDCPA and Fair credit billing act discuss those violations.

You are probably thinking by now well HOW DO I START WHAT DO I DO? Start by studying consistently. Just like most scroll on social media all day, revert the energy into studying. Think for a moment, you just found out laws after studying regarding your car payment being fraudulently collected the entire time and the law says you can get all that money back what do you think you should do? ASK FOR IT! Simple! It is not rocket science unless you have not studied. I am not talking 4 - 6 months, this knowledge requires years! Some may say that it takes too long to study, they don't have time, or these laws don't work. Well you been lied to all your life and you cannot study? Those kinds of statements come from a slave mentality person. The same person that will tell you these laws do not work are the same ones scamming you with templates and regurgitated information they tried to copy while learning from me. Everything I have clarified for a client I can find in federal law. It makes so much sense to use their federal definitions vs black law dictionary as most "gurus" will use and swear by it. Then you have people that use memes to try to teach you lol. One thing everyone knows about me is I know these laws off the top of my head. I do not use any notes when I am teaching 5 hours at a time. It is all in my head from years of studying. I always get asked what law school I went to lol. No lawyer will ever go into detail on the record with these laws because these laws say they are not attorneys but debt collectors. So those FDCPA attorneys are smoke screens and mirrors telling consumers they only entitled to $1000.00. The lies they tell pursuant to 15 USC 1692k. Even though I have a B.S degree in Criminal Justice I was never taught any of these laws. So, it is exactly what it is called BS!

Now let's get to remedy. I am old school and it is wise to put everything in writing never over the phone (the FDCPA tell you that as well). These people have been harassing you for years over something that never belonged to them CREDIT. 18 USC 8 tells us all obligations are for the UNITED STATES not the natural person. Then 28 USC 3002 (15) tells us the United States is federal corporation under the Judiciary laws. If you ever been served with a lawsuit, you may have seen what they call an Affidavit which is a sworn statement of facts. If anyone opposes or attempts to create an obligation for me, I complete an affidavit with my sworn facts and make them PROVE IT. An unrebutted affidavit stands as the truth in commerce and results in a default judgement pursuant to the Federal rules of civil procedure rule 55 or summary judgement under rule 56. Please pay close attention to the civil remedy under the FDCPA regarding jurisdiction. One key word ENFORCE not ARGUE. No one can tell you how to be a parent to your child because you know who you are as a parent.   that ENERGY along with 15 USC 1692c(d). So if you get to a point and do not know what to do that is because you do not know who you are! Nothing more nothing less. There are so many layers to this, which is why most continue being a slave to America vs being the creditor they are.

TESTIMONIALS

" As soon as I said I was a consumer in traffic court for a DWI, the court reporter stopped typing and the judge mouth dropped, I never seen that Envi, the case was continued. (this person never got a new court date everything disappeared)

"Envi, Capital One settled with me for 20k!!" Thank you so much for your clarity and praise to your ancestors.

"All we said was everything here is false and misleading puruant to 15 USC 1692e" Next thing we know the DA won't talk to us anymore and her name was no longer on the court docket, she walked out no charges after being in jail for 4 days for felony larceny".

"Good Day Empress,
I wanted to share my cousins experience with you in traffic court. He received a summons for not fully stopping at Stop sign. I told him to plead not guilty and indicate he would be accompanied by his counsel of choice. This was a letter I wrote on his behalf along with the summons submitted. First I have to say we were shocked the Traffic Violation accepted this, so for him that was our first victory.
Once we were in front of the judge we had to ask multiple times to speak, they just want you to say yes, I understand and pay the fine. I told him to ask the judge ..what did I do wrong, please explain in detail? Once the judge explained,, he went on to ask...As a consumer I was simply traveling and unaware it was possible to be

17

liable...This made everyone quiet...they ask my nervous cousin to repeat it hoping he would stumble, when he repeated it, you could tell now his confidence stood behind his words and the court room was so quiet I was scared...lol

The judge proceeded to speak to him sarcastically and reminded him he had been to traffic court before. I made my cousin say I was unaware of who I was and the federal laws that protect me. Once he stated this the woman who sits in front of the judge went over to the judge and spoke with him briefly before telling him this was dismissed. The officer who had previously arrested my cousin months ago and also pulled him over for the summons made an inappropriate comment. My cousin at this point feeling himself said outloud, this is the officer who kidnapped me and 16 other men. I feel targeted...the judge just looked at him and then the officer, who was in shock and pissed the judge didn't shut him down for making the statement. The judge reminded my cousin the traffic violation was dismissed and we ran out of there as fast as possible once he received his paperwork indicating dismissed.

I want to thank you for sharing your overstanding of Consumer Law. This has changed my life and the life of my family. Grateful to you always."

1:40 PM

Peace Envi, the court granted my default judgment in my case as of Monday so I wanted to thank you for sharing the information that I needed.

Midland Credit Management
350 Camino De La Reina
Suite 100
San Diego, CA 92108

877-382-5063

5/3/2021

Original Credit
Original Account Number
MCM Account Number
Current Owner
Current Se
Current Ba

@scaleinc
@magickbynature

Thank you for your recent communication. We have reviewed our records and are writing to provide the following update:

We have closed your account and ceased collections. You have no further obligation regarding this account.

Please call Consumer Support Services at 877-382-6063 if you have any additional questions.

Se habla espanol: 877-898-3955

Sincerely,

Tim Bohn
Consumer Support Services

DEFINITIONS

DEFINTIONS UNDER THE CONSUMER PROTECTION LAWS- These are scrambled throughout title 15 Chapter 41. Study, Study, Study . You owe it to yourself to get everything back they took from you!

1. The term "consumer" means any natural person obligated or allegedly obligated to pay any debt.
2. The term "creditor" means any person who offers or extends credit creating a debt or to whom a debt is owed, but such term does not include any person to the extent that he receives an assignment or transfer of a debt in default solely for the purpose of facilitating collection of such debt for another.
3. The term "debt" means any obligation or alleged obligation of a consumer to pay money arising out of a transaction in which the money, property, insurance, or services which are the subject of the transaction are primarily for personal, family, or household purposes, whether or not such obligation has been reduced to judgment.
4. The term "person" means a natural person or an organization.
5. The term "credit" means the right granted by a creditor to a debtor to defer payment of debt or to incur debt and defer its payment.
6. The adjective "consumer", used with reference to a credit transaction, characterizes the transaction as one in which the party to whom credit is offered or extended

is a natural person, and the money, property, or services which are the subject of the transaction are primarily for personal, family, or household purposes.

7. The term "credit card" means any card, plate, coupon book or other credit device existing for the purpose of obtaining money, property, labor, or services on credit.

8. The term "consumer credit transaction" means any transaction in which credit is offered or extended to an individual for personal, family, or household purposes.

9. the term "business day" means any day on which the offices of the consumer's financial institution involved in an electronic fund transfer are open to the public for carrying on substantially all of its business functions;

10. the term "financial institution" means a State or National bank, a State or Federal savings and loan association, a mutual savings bank, a State or Federal credit union, or any other person who, directly or indirectly, holds an account belonging to a consumer;

11. The term "applicant" means any person who applies to a creditor directly for an extension, renewal, or continuation of credit, or applies to a creditor indirectly by use of an existing credit plan for an amount exceeding a previously established credit limit.

Again, I hope you all begin to study so you can see it for yourself none of this is made up. It is ok to have an opinion on federal laws you did not create whether you want to believe them or not. Just overstand when you comply with other laws that have noting to do with you such as traffic, child support etc but oppose these you are the problem not the law. I have a online academy for consumers to partake in if they choose. You can visit youtube type in MONEY BAG TOUR and you can check out the highlight reels! I will continue to give clarity in all areas the ancestors lead me to. SCALE INC & MAGICK BY NAYTURE are my businssess that make this possible as well.

I may have been imitated but never duplicated. You will see "celebrities" talking about this publicy after they took my classes. As a public disclosure ENVI IS THE ONLY ONE WITH THE MONEY BAG TOUR, CREATED BY MY ANCESTORS. There have been many trying to associate my legit business with there hobby lol. If you DID NOT hear me say it believe me it's false. I did make poor choices on attemting to allow others to expand their business by joining me on my tours but the ancestors said NO. I move with integrity and grace. I have a low tolerance for scammers, liars and bullies.

"IF YOU KNOW WHO YOU ARE YOU KNOW WHAT TO DO" ~ENVI

ABOUT THE AUTHOR

Envi

Envi earned her B.S degree in Criminal Just-
ice in 2005. Envi is a fiery motivated inspir-
ing wife and mother of three. She analyzes
everything from laws to nutrition. In 2010,
she found herself homeless with a toddler
and pregnant as a single mom. Through
prayer and meditation, she found a spiritual
mentor who guided her to what her life pur-
pose was to uplift fallen humanity. She went from being homeless
to giving hope!

Made in the USA
Las Vegas, NV
27 June 2021